T0106343

Powerful Poetry
for Local Hearts

JAMES MICHAEL DAVIES

authorHOUSE®

AuthorHouse™
1663 Liberty Drive
Bloomington, IN 47403
www.authorhouse.com
Phone: 1-800-839-8640

© 2012 by James Michael Davies. All rights reserved.

No part of this book may be reproduced, stored in a retrieval system, or transmitted by any means without the written permission of the author.

First published by AuthorHouse   01/24/2012

ISBN: 978-1-4678-8417-4 (sc)
ISBN: 978-1-4678-8418-1 (ebk)

Printed in the United States of America

Any people depicted in stock imagery provided by Thinkstock are models, and such images are being used for illustrative purposes only.
Certain stock imagery © Thinkstock.

This book is printed on acid-free paper.

Because of the dynamic nature of the Internet, any web addresses or links contained in this book may have changed since publication and may no longer be valid. The views expressed in this work are solely those of the author and do not necessarily reflect the views of the publisher, and the publisher hereby disclaims any responsibility for them.

Contents

Messenger

I'm the harbinger I bring news everybody stops and listens to
me because I have something to say,
You will stop and hear me you must,
I know you will anyway because you are credulous.

I have the information you yearn,
The desire you have to find out is a deep burn,
I can tell this from you because of the vehement you show
towards me,
You are becoming impatient, restless, and shaking or maybe it
is because you are cantankerous.

Guess what though . . . .
I'm not going to tell you,
I like this hold I have on you,
I know it's a pain in the cranium,
But to me it is really fun!

Museum

Walking around I search, ponder and absorb the information
and models which surround me,
A museum with a plethora of information from history.

The swansong of many things,
The invention of others, the gong,
All gone? Most gone?
Dodo, T-Rex swansong?

I look at the building walls, doors, and floors age makes the
quality look suddenly shoddy, an antique itself.

The swansong of many,
Others crumble others fall the museum sees it all,
All gone? Most gone?
Post office, corner shop swansong?

I look at the explanations of the articles a perspicacious look
at dinosaurs allegedly to of been walloped by a comet at the
populations summit only then to be swathe for millions of
years in tar, oil e.t.c before being exposed to us all.

The swansong of many,
Dinosaurs are one twin towers another,
All gone? Most gone?
Tigers, elephants, mustang swansong?

James Michael Davies

It's a . . .

Big, heavy a true giant,
Grins with evil like a salesman to a client,
Head and shoulders above the rest,
It's a metallic, make-shift, mad, mess.

Trees turn to twigs,
Sheep the size of figs,
Close to the house make them look like boxes,
It looks down at critters with disgust especially foxes.

A display of monumental hatred,
Its presence will never be faded.

Yes indeed the pylon is not very friendly.

TEXT !?

Y do u wryt in sch a wy?
Wats up wit jus usin th fone,
Thts wat it is 4.
Its quik n svs mney.
Wat eva hppned 2 pst?
Nt needed technology hs developed.
Txt is ere 2 sty so use it.
NO
Y do u wryt in sch a wy?

P.C   (Personal Confusion)

Square structural stiff,
A glorified jack in the box,
As the screen blazes,
Tasks can be like mazes.

But like a lion can be tamed,
By the people who can't be named,
It is an iconic building a piece of the future.

It holds the answers too many questions,
It holds the weapons for many wars,
It has the potential to unlock many doors,
Many people have it within their walls.

Projection of ones soul

Even though one practices, performs and presents skills to help and achieve to build bridges and reputation one cannot shake the overwhelming reality of loneliness.

If only they knew the emptiness within,
If only they knew the love trapped within,
If only they knew the weakness within.

If my state of individual misery could be shared if only for a moment, the release would be greater than the worse type of torture known.

James Michael Davies

Easter- lost in translation

The once beaten, suffering Christ has now been replaced by the bouncing seasonal rabbit.

The deeper meaning with roots to the saviour of all people has now been replaced by an explosive message of cheap chocolate.

Other-Worldly

I stand and gaze into the mirror,
What I see is not a reflection,
But a portal to a parallel world,
The more I look the more I see,
Faces from the present, behind me those from the past,
My pupils widen until they engulf my eyes and become a vortex,
Soon the boundaries of reality become faded to the point I can hear voices,
And my surroundings seem to change,
Suddenly a mysterious figure touches me,
I am back in front of the mirror.

The search

Inspiration can be found,
In every person, in every town.

From the polished cobbles of the British village,
To the harsh rocks and sands of the third world.

You could lounge in the tropics and absorb the overwhelming
chorus of exotic wildlife music notes,
Or simply observe the traditional continuous, downpour of
home as it creates streams along the roads.

The journey for inspiration can take you south or can take you
west,
But deep in you is often best.

Christmas again

A robin at Christmas sits on my fence amongst the snow that lies along the top and its breast,
A small ball of feathers,
I look at the rest of the garden scanning for more small critters,
As I blow the steam from my hot chocolate leaving condensation on my upper lip,
It shares a similar vision as my cake with thick white icing,
I stare harder through my steamy window and notice small imprints from the top to the bottom of the garden,
They seem to be them of a bird but I know from which bird, my small robin,
I step back from the extreme heat of the radiator,
He sees me move and shivers and flies away with the white powder falling from its beating wings,
I change the location I search and ponder,
The gutter of a house shows numerous clear needles I see one fall and smash near where I once knew grass,
I retreat to my final place there is tinsel over a tree with presents to bring glee,
A log fuelled fire something I much desire,
Tinsel, streamers and a nativity with three wise men,
These all tell me its Christmas again.

James Michael Davies

Peony rose

An explosion of colour,
A fulfilment of pleasure,
Vibrant flowers,
Fresh lush leaves fill it out,
A sudden centre piece of the garden.

As I look it speaks no jargon,
Only a simple story of basic words,
A plant fit for royalty,
As it is not novelty.

Only strong in still conditions,
As the winds rush in,
Its structure buckles and collapses,
But leaves the promise,
It'll return bounteous next spring.

The moon

Their was a lad,
They said he was mad,
And never was very glad,

Because suddenly one noon,
Out came the moon,
And it would turn him into a fool.

He jumped up and down,
Never a frown,
And he played the clown.

But when the moon went in,
He turned very dim,
Because people got fed up of him.

James Michael Davies

Summer break

Sun,
Sea,
Sand,
Summer,
I can't wait.

Ice-cream,
Laughter,
Sun cream,
Fun,
I can't wait.

Teachers,
Education,
Lessons,
School,
I can wait.

Depresivision

The dull television instantly bored,
Whilst my father tunefully snores,
Rubbish programs increase more and more,
As empty beer cans lie on the floor.

The small screen now seems to be,
Full of pathetic celebrity,
Whether they can swim, fly or scream,
Is of no interest to me.

Whatever happened to the days when,
The box wasn't dominated by football and Sven,
Exciting times and programs of back then,
I fear will never occur again.

James Michael Davies

Calm before the storm

The once blue sky which whistled an uplifting tune,
Is now a mass of grey, bloated matter that groans a miserable boom.

The streets are now deserted leaving the effect of an abandoned wasteland.

The birds now do not sing and fly,
But take shelter, huddle and sigh.

No sound exists but the pace of the wind has increased and is now constant,
Any relief of this atmosphere will be a godsend.

Suddenly the sky split, cracked and ruptured thousands upon millions of raindrops descend towards the roads, gardens and paths,
Each of them making an individual splash.

Rivers run the tarmac while puddles sit on grass,
Then everything ceases,
As the sun and sky come back to whistle,
And nothing is miserable.

Bullies

Their bigger than me,
There are more of them than me,
They hurt more than me.

They rob me,
They hurt me,
They hate me.

I only got a better score,
I only talk to the teacher,
I only bring my equipment.

Why me?
Why am I sad?
Why am I here?

James Michael Davies

Black tulip

Head and shoulders above the rest,
Fighting coldness to be the best,
Taking time to expose its flower,
Overwhelming strength shows its power.

Slow at growing, takes its time,
But when it does it almost shines,
As the cold weather and trouble comes,
It stands its ground straight and proud.

And even when the rest have gone,
It refuses to go and be gone,
Because it has stood their and has shone,
Its stubborn attitude is foregone,
But now it will disappear only to reappear, but its trooping
character makes this poem a brilliant sonnet.

A whole different world

Thousands of proud blades deep as the roots which are released to secure the sturdy anchorage in the earth is the colour it withholds,
Army green.

Emphasising this beautiful wave of unity is glorious parades of bright and unusual colour, products from the soldiers standing dignified In line forming a powerful mass border.

Foreign bodies invade from air beyond the boundaries only to land in the water provided by a structure build for this purpose.

Suddenly,

More and more appear the guards take immediate action to clear the area the four legs and growling teeth are enough to bring peace and justice once more.

Clearly ones garden is a magnificent characterised place.

Cat eat bird

Between my finger and my thumb,
The thin pencil lies, snug as a bug.

Under my window I hear a mysterious ruffling sound,
Its feathers press against the cold pavement,
It's a blackbird taking cover, I stare.

Eventually his shaking body lays adjacent to the floor,
My mind flashes back 5 years.

A cat prowling spots his dinner,
A bird feeding as if to simmer.

The sharp claws sink into the fence,
The top edging against the hind leg was pressed firmly,
He blocked out all surroundings and raised his long tail high,
To get perfect balance that is so crucial,
Keeping perfectly still as the clear blue sky in summer.

The old tom could hunt birds,
Just like his old man.

That cat slaughtered more prey in one day,
Than any other tom within 6 miles of him,
Once I presented a bowl of milk to him,
His ears pricked straight up to attention and drained the
bowl,
Just as if it had a hole in the bottom,
Then he dashed straight away to start his work again,

Jumping and climbing up old giant trees to sleep or just to spy
on prey going up and up to find the highest points, climbing.
The silent movements of the cat,
The wittiness and awareness of the blackbird,
The quick movements of the bird,
Leaves a disappointed, alone cat,
This bird wasn't going to get caught; every bird has its day.
The flying feathers awaken me,
But I've no feathers to save me like them I've not tail to keep
me balanced like them.

Between my finger and my thumb,
The thin pencil lies. IL survive with it.

James Michael Davies

Come cycle

Come we me cycle,
Come with me quick,
Come with me through meadows,
Come through the streets.

Together we will cycle,
Together we will see,
Smell the wild flowers,
Along the crashing blue sea.

With the sun on our shoulders,
And breeze through our hair,
The night will soon come to stop and scare,
(But the moonlight makes you look fairer).

So come cycle my darling,
Come cycle with me,
Come cycle my beauty because I love thee.

Regulation 30: living in terror

My garden, it once seemed a pleasant retreat,
Especially in the summer when blue tits would tweet,
I remember one time when me and some mates would laugh
and run about with bare feet.

But no more . . . .
That was a long time ago,
How can such a great memory also feel so sore?
I used to smile each time I looked upon my garden, so full and
lush . . . . now just a miserable baron shadow.

I am of course writing about regulation 30,
So carelessly named as they don't realise so many people are
hurting.

And you of course know to what I refer,
As do so many people out there,
It is on TV. And the papers,
And if you are reading this then it must have been pulled from
my cold lifeless fingers.

And I am dead . . . .
As this book is my last friend.

Well if I am dead the least I could do,
Is tell you all of how it begun, then you'll understand it could
happen to you.

It happened at a sudden and a crash one day,
Nobody would of guessed it would happen this way,

It seemed like an explosion, an eruption of rock,
Out of a cliff and could be seen from Whitby dock.

It happened at plain sight,
Not even at night!
Everyone who seen it ran in sheer fright.

It thumped and it smashed a very long way,
Through lots of towns and past Whitley bay,
 It was even seen running on the moors one day,
But closer and faster it came this way.

Now many people including me,
Would not believe this even in a story,
If only we acted to what we seen,
Instead of leaving it to the army.

I remember watching the news saying that can't be,
That creature only exists in myth and poetry.

At this point I should say regulation 30,
Killed me and many others,
Just to save the majority of the country,
Abandoned by our government,
Left as bait with no hope or food.

Another fine memory I have again watching the news,
The official report of the creatures' latest moves,
It included a report containing its name,
This didn't come as a shock for some as through myth and
history it had gained much fame,
But may not be stereotypically the same.

For the creature in real life had huge teeth,
And even when running towered countless feet,

It had very pale skin but smelt like rot,
And one huge piercing eye it was of course a Cyclops.

For days the Cyclops ran rampage,
Covering miles with one short run,
Little did we know the misery had just begun,
The army really tried its best,
But still with wounds the Cyclops refused to rest.

Until the end of the week,
The Cyclops slowed and started to bleed,
With a shot from a tank which landed between its feet.

. . . . The Cyclops was brought to its knees,
But not killed too injured to walk but from orders kept sedate
the locals were not too pleased,
Riots and fights fast occurred,
The army's attention soon became too blurred.

The fights and battles grew fast and fierce,
The innocent people pleaded but they could not hear us,
The town of Thornaby slowly was turning to dust,
The population rapidly dispersed,
At least those wealthy enough some went east some went
west.

Until only a small population was left and, the consistent
presence of army soldiers and scientist who continued with
their persistent experiments on the creature.

It's been one whole month since the Cyclops first fell to the
ground,
Already the population is down to one thousand,
The riots and wars have destroyed all and once green things
are now brown.

James Michael Davies

Dear reader I am stuck within a stalemate,
It consists of the few people left behind but too poor and afraid to move,
A now baron wasteland that once used to soothe,
The soldiers and officials who keep guard in case the unimaginable happens,
And finally the forever threatening presence of the sedated Cyclops.

One vital detail I forgot to mention,
While the army had idle days a strong barricade was made to keep the beast within,
Which on one fine day (or as good as can be),
A terrible thing occurred which brings me to this day.

As fast as a blink the Cyclops awoke,
Chains and equipment he violently broke,
Slowly and grouchy from his knees he arose,
Quickly and effectively soldiers and scientists he battled,
Until his immediate surroundings crumbled.

Until finally only a small army number was left behind,
The others did retreat to tell the government that they could not fight,
Now I and a few others are hiding at the mercy of the Cyclops in the hope he will not escape his boundaries.

Once the government received word the Cyclops was conscience again it ruled "it would be too expensive to maintain security of this beast and too many good men have been lost nobody is to go near, into or outside the boundaries of Thornaby the beast will soon die of hunger as we believe the boundaries built for it are sufficient our thoughts are with the locals of Thornaby"

This ruling was later believed to of been made to reduce bad publicity for the government, save money and save army resources and was named . . . . regulation 30.

This first hand story was recovered from a crash site within Thornaby in the form of a diary, no known survivors were found, the Cyclops was allowed to escape and has never been seen since.

The barn that time forgot

A glorious field rolled high along the horizon,
Masked by the early morning fog,
The glowing red sun burns away the screen,
This reveals a barn that time forgot.

Beads of fog residue can clearly be seen slowly sliding down
the large stone walls,
The once strong beams now warped through time,
Streaks of light cut through the air inside,
As it pushes past the missing tiles.

And the only life that now exists,
Are the simplest creatures that you might even miss,
Three small harvest mice snuggled in hay,
Protected from the troubles that killed the farm that day.

The cost of ignorance

Once there lived a group of boos, nimble creatures,
Inert heart, empty face and a crippled figure made up their features.

Amongst them existed an elder hoodwink who based his life upon pettifogging but due to petulance amongst the boos towards the hoodwink brought terrible hoodoo,
Your terribly prolix and full of hoodoo said the chief boo.

Your pettifogging has got out of hand,
So at once I banish you from this land.

At haste he retreated and against the cold ground his feet beating,
But now nobody did his job checking the dry wood and monitoring the petrol to make sure the two don't mix.

The area got neglected untidy and very unkindly,
A young boo made at two a terrible hoodoo as at once the gas and wood combust ending in the most terrible inferno the whole of boo town has ever seen since they established in 1816 all of the boos perished and fried apart from the one who was watching from miles.

Don't make the same mistake as the boos,
Never let small hoodoos,
Distract you from the big picture of life,
Make sure you always go to bed with a clear conscience at night.

James Michael Davies

The maid and the banister

An old Victorian house,
Stood still through time,
The same family of mouse,
A overgrown garden with herbs and thyme.

Inside the house beneath the old wooden beams,
A young maid walks and begins to sweep,

The banister shines, the floors are clean and the cutlery is polished so it gleams.

She works without thanks all day to night,
When she is finished she stays out of sight,
Walking up through the winding dark wooden stairs,
Past the biggest rooms until she finds hers.

The banister shines, the floors are clean and the cutlery is polished so it gleams.

When the morning comes she feels so alone,
The kitchen is very large and open plan,
Breakfast is served as fast as she can.

The banister shines, the floors are clean and the cutlery is polished so it gleams.

The family she serves comes down at last,
Seemingly wealthy and definitely greedy they scoff the breakfast faster than fast,
She takes one look at the mess and lets out a sigh,
The family leaves the house without a simple goodbye.

The banister shines, the floors are clean and the cutlery is polished so it gleams.

Here is where her life takes a twist,
Straddling her iron push bike she cycles to the local baker`s,
Her wheels whizz along winding country lanes which lead to cobbled town streets, the scenery around just a mist,
Through the window food is surrounded by the frantic bread makers.

The banister shines, the floors are clean and the cutlery is polished so it gleams.

The bell rings above her head as she enters the store,
Her eyes look at one particular man,
And tries to get his attention as she has done before,
They both discreetly exit through the back into the old olive green van.

The banister shines, the floors are clean and the cutlery is polished so it gleams.

They are secretive lover`s who enjoy bursts of time together,
They would drive away in his van to stop and lie amongst the heather,
Her secret pleasure,
An escape from her unforgiving, miserable life,
And now he will ask her to be his wife.

The banister shines, the floors are clean and the cutlery is polished so it gleams.

On the way back home they drive past fields,
Both lost in thought by the way they feel,
Man and lady happy in love,
There hearts glowing together as the radiant sun above.

James Michael Davies

The banister shines, the floors are clean and the cutlery is polished so it gleams.

The baker sees time just like him had suddenly slipped away,
For months they have been lucky to be back on time but maybe not today,
The massive rubbers of the van tear along the road,
The baker's ambition started to become too bold.

The banister shines, the floors are clean and the cutlery is polished so it gleams.

With their private happy life threatened or so they feel,
The baker's hands tightened upon the wheel,
A bead of sweat down his forehead,
A trembling tear drips past her neck,
A littered narrow lane ahead proves too much for one balding tyre tread.

Back at the manor a single rusty leaf blows in and is left,
The floor looses its shine and is left,
An official, unrespectable letter on the kitchen top for the maid is left,
Due to complicated taxes the family had been summoned, sentenced and left.

The floors now dim; the cutlery glum the antique banister still shines strong.

A destroyed smoking Ford lay upside down on a remote country lane,
Inside two people who will never live again,
A young maid with a guilty conscience a tear still rolling down one cheek,

And a young baker with sweat on his brow with a new grip now so weak.

The floors now dim; the cutlery glum the antique banister still shines strong.

At her manor her soul returns,
A guilty ghost cleans the stairs,
Trying not to let the family know,
She had been meeting her lover instead of being home,
Until she notices some strangers leave,
She listens to them talking then saw a letter, she begun to read.

The floors now dim; the cutlery glum the antique banister still shines strong.

The letter did say:
To the household and those inside,
You owe much money to thy,
Bring yourself and the staff you pay,
Down to the station rapidly,
Your taxes are wrong your debts are high,
Please do this without delay I will be much obliged.
The maid looked up and felt free as before and left through the light to find her lover once more.

The floors are now dusty the cutlery is gone,
A black iron push bike still stands alone,
Nobody knows for sure how the two did go,
But two small moths sit side by side on the shiniest banister of all.

James Michael Davies

Two girls

There are two girls in this world,
They are moving as fast as they can go,
But the world around them goes so slow,
The only secure thing the know,
Is at night they are alone.

That's when they dream of something new,
They love their Mam and Dad,
They want us so they are down on their knees praying and
asking.

Everyday their disappointment they are masking,
We never see them but they are always trying to play,
Show us the way,
Show us how to be really here,
With skin you can touch and feel,
And so you can see us,
We want to be real,
You should listen to us because,
We were meant to be your daughters.

A place of inspiration

A bulbous metallic hub which runs from the energy of every passionate workers heart within.

The muscle from the labourers,
The brains of the platers and pipe-fitters,
The accuracy of the burners,
The flawless gleam from the cleaners in every area,
Whilst the welders input keeps everything together,
Makes the place run from one year to another,
With the unity of one worker, to the other,

All this and the continuous upbeat, hardworking attitude of every individual gives this place of work a fantastic atmosphere.

Money may be slack,
And times may be sad,
And if I ever got the sack,
I would hope to be invited back.

James Michael Davies

A word about life

I'm told your best years,
Are your younger years?
Spent fooling around and chasing girls,
Sometimes scuffling and getting jailed.

I'm told in your adult years,
Time is spent working and chasing girls,
Working and having a girl,
And giving them money.

I can't wait till my older years,
When iv got girls chasing me for money,
And I can pretend to be deaf when they ask for it.

Accident

When the sky was just black satin with glitter,
And the air was still bitter,
My stomach seemed to jitter.

I saw the old man lying there,
I seemed to stand and stare,
Other pedestrians did not care.

The screaming siren came,
And took the man away,
Then the car carried on,
As if the man was never down.

When the sky turns to black satin with glitter,
My stomach begins to jitter,
That's when I see him.

James Michael Davies

After work

I put on my slippers and casually throw some more wood on
the fire,
The roaring flames in front of me eliminates the cold from
beyond the window,
I squeeze half an orange into my gin and sink into my green
leather armchair.

I engage into staring and concentration as my inferno speaks
to me in cracks and flicks,
While holding on to my beverage from which I take sips,
Suddenly a song disturbs me,
I hunt for its source only to discover birds in a tree,
Singing so light and free.

As I retreat I notice a small hedgehog taking minute steps as it
twitches around sniffing the air what it senses I don't know,
My gin and orange I need more!

Choices choices

So many options, so many chances,
Many people choose to be a musical and become famous through dances,
Others a more physical career using bricks and mortar,
Some are more academic with words and paper but still hard work (sorter).

But

What would happen if one were to suddenly switch career,
Use more brain and drink less beer,
What if I chased a passion, followed a dream in order to find my true self,
And have a career that would put me on the map and off the shelf.

And

This new venture will take away the life so dim,
In exchange for a life in film,
Exaggeration may be present but necessary in order for possibility to exist.

In conclusion

Things will remain untouched,
The alternative not butchered,
But kept close as plan B,
That is good enough for me,

James Michael Davies

Grinders at work

The sound of grinders all around me,
In attempt to deafen me,
To clean the metal and obtain symmetry,
Without the use of chemistry.

The sparks drift from the disc as dragonflies on a summers
midnight,
The sound resembles the atmosphere of a severe cat-fight,
At the end of each run a fresh layer of glistening dust lays upon
the ground.

But still amongst the apparent harsh treatment,
A bond exists between man and machine,
This makes the metal component an exotic creation,
This scene fused with welding produces a magnificent display
of colour, unity and passion.

Here and then

A stroll in the park can often be,
A relaxing and thoughtful time for me,
Hand in hand we walk along,
With each other we belong.

We breathe the air,
And have no care,
We look to the distance the weather looks more fair,
Guided by the sun we will go there.

We reach the lake,
In it there is ducks which glide and skate,
We sit in some close shade,
I notice two old faces looking back from the water but soon
fade.

James Michael Davies

Home work

I'm sorry miss I don't have it,
Well find it boy,
I'm sorry miss I did have it,
Well get it back boy,
I'm sorry miss my fish ate it,
Well bring the fish,
I'm sorry miss my bird ate the fish,
Well bring the bird,
I'm sorry miss the cat ate the bird,
Well bring the cat,
I'm sorry miss my dog ate the cat,
Well bring the dog,
I'm sorry miss my dog was ran over by a speeding car,
I'm sorry boy I killed your dog.

In the country

A fly gently and cautiously manoeuvres around the
circumference of the daisy,
 And then to more flowers, very hasty,
As the soft, radiant glow of the sunbeam strokes each individual
petal.

The sun itself seems to smile agreeably with nature's current
way.

WHOOSH!

A car as fast as the insect with the occupants on the phone
flies by,
The metal, noisy, monster turns the landscape to a dirty, gritty,
fog,
The once heavenly glow now a collection of gravel and fag
ash.

The sun is now a grey void which now frowns at the world.

James Michael Davies

Just work

The arrogant roar of the motors,
The unmerciful, sharp components,
Which is the dangerous machinery used, not only to shape the
final product but also my future.

Everyday I witness the constant screeching and cracking of
metal working against metal,
A never ending display of sparks, flashes and noise.

I join in myself grabbing a machine to clean up a weld just as
one would grab a wild bull by its horns.

Small droplets of sweat slowly develop on my already hot
forehead before running into each eyebrow,
Like a tap dripping into a bowl where they come to rest,
As I step back and look at my finished structure of weld, metal
and effort.

Morn to night

The horizon is a fire,
The sky a glorious display from the aura of the flames presenting a blanket of red, orange, yellow,
Trees bushes and houses simply silhouettes,
The scene brings a feeling of relaxation and ambience.

When morning comes the glowing sky turns to a graduation of black to blue,
In company with embedded diamonds and the haunting enchanting glow of the moon.

Before the morning birds come out and sing bringing in a fresh new start which gently melts the sitting frost upon the tree branches.

James Michael Davies

Moving home diaries

The first step of leaving home,
Pack your bags say farewell off you go,
New surroundings different rooms,
The prospect of being a man looms.

After a week or so different jobs occur,
I don't mind doing them because I love her,
Different jobs I have always done,
But all help seems to be gone.

I do jobs in my new house,
In hope to gain some nouse,
I love feeling like a man,
Doing the gardening,
I also love living with my girlfriend.

Riding home

I finish work and wrap up warm,
I put on my new overall,
Bright and reflective I add my lights,
Suitable attire for these dark nights,
I start on my way through the dark, tornado winds and typhoon rains,
Across the black ice that causes so much fright,
On occasions lay white crisp snow which crunch under my tires,
Disturbing the blanket that lay before me I glance back to see my track,
It marks my route tomorrow I shall follow it to find my way back.

But I am prepared for this weather and all it bears my scarf protects my face my woolly hat and hood protects the rest of my head I wear a armour like coat impenetrable from the outside to protect my torso and gloves to protect my hands as these are vulnerable to the elements now I am the soldier and the storm is my enemy as I am dressed for battle.

The rain lashes me while the wind blows me off course as the ice and snow attack my transport to try and get me to the floor where I would lay in a helpless pile but I fight and progress.

James Michael Davies

I brace the storm the last few yards to reach my home a storm that Ares would be proud of or one that he would create as he is god of war and is murderous, bloodstained and disliked by many just like the storm which causes pain and inconvenience but also like Ares is cowardly.

I finally make a heroes return home but the cold has made me raw,
I settle into the warmth and get ready for tomorrows war.

Saving

Save water,
Save money,
Save food,
Keep waste,
Recycle.

Save your time,
Save your advice,
I need to live,
This is not the 3rd world.

Sometimes

Often when reflecting upon the past the memories become
more pleasant than the truth,
People seem to be happy and places seem to be comforting,
Sometimes,
Colours become vivid, voices more acoustic but,
Modern life distracts us from reality,
And prevents us from enjoying day to day life sometimes,
Our perception of truth interferes,
With reality.

The change

Slow and grotty is my mind,
Something wild and eventful will help I find,
I think and ponder of what I can do,
Surely exercise will improve mind and muscle.

I get out my weights and pump iron,
I get out my trainers and make tracks,
I get out my schedule which I will follow for weeks.

Not before long I see a change,
I feel a change overall as cool as a fridge,
Then I see, I notice sharpness, quickness but most of all increased strength as much as a bridge,
I'm becoming buff and I like it its here to stay this is the change.

The park

I sit on this bench all alone,
As I gaze across the vast green field in front,
The blades of grass sway in harmony as the cool breeze drifts
along and whistles around my ears.

I let the soft glow of the sun gently caress my cheeks and
arms,
Whilst in the distance children play on the swings and others
climb a tree,
I hear them all laughing with glee.

I also hear within the breeze,
The sweet, cheerful songs of birds also in the trees,
I sit alone on this bench but other people I do not miss,
I am in company with my local nature and it is truly bliss.

Through life

When becoming of age certain things make up memories that we treasure such as.

Running home from school as the crisp snow crunches under each foot,
Observing the stars above for the first time which resembles glitter across a blank, black canvass.

That party when you first got drunk,
You might have even been a punk,
Those are times you should remember when life seems to be a load of junk,
And you feel down,
Because those happy moments are always with you and around.

Typical!

To me my experiences are both typical and unlucky,
To others they seem both hysterical and funny,
Why these things happen to me is a mystery,
To others they happen and become history,
But not me I end up having to dwell,
Like that time I ended up at the bottom of a well!

In the house I take a walk, I need a folk,
But all I find is a knife and a spoon . . .
And of course I'm in the wrong room!
This is a habit I should sort.

I go outside and clean up after dogs I don't own,
As I need to get rid of the reminder from my shoe . . . .
I become ill from smokers cough,
Because of the way the smoke drifts around me as if to mock,
I don't smoke, but look at those who do and scoff.

But ill carry on tidying up others mess,
As that's what I seem to do best!
I start to cook my tea as I wonder,
If a day will go by without a blunder,
As I realise I've set alight my jumper.

What a day

Basking in the glory of the wonderful warmth,
Smelling the gorgeous aroma of the angels amongst the weeds
with names more exotic than the flowers than the flowers
they actually withhold African violets, cactus, and orchids.

Whilst at the same time observing the wildlife consuming the
lush treats that I placed on the cap of my fence blue tits, green
finch, and sparrows.

But every up has its down,
I swing at flies because they make me frown,
But still they swarm,
Then peace is broken as my dad mows the lawn,
Suddenly I'm as disorientated as the new pattern the green
blades now present.

What a day!

James Michael Davies

50 years

An old lady and older gentleman,
Sat hand in hand watching the sea,
As the waves gently lapped against the shore,
Their minds are transported to a time long ago.

A time when they too were young,
And when their relationship had just begun,
He would impress her and pamper,
So that he could see her smile and hear her laughter.

They would dance and lay upon the beach,
While the older couples watched.

An old lady and older gentleman,
Sat hand in hand watching the sea,
As a young woman and man walked past as the young woman
glanced over and thought "I wish that will be me".

A night in

One full year we have been together a thoughtful layout I have prepared,
Candle light table with chicken and a luxurious desert as we stare lovingly to each other,
Hand in hand thumb to thumb.

We would share never-ending moments together,
We would have no desire to be anywhere else,
We would go over the past year and remember the best.

After dinner we share a drink stronger than water and cuddle into each other while watching our TV.

James Michael Davies

Being you

I'm curious what It is you do,
What's it like being with you,
How do you do things and move,
I dream of what it would be like,
To be the person you are even though you are a,
Alternate species but not a dog,
But a fish gracefully gliding,
Around in your environment without,
A care or worry even though you have no legs,
It is the freedom you have which I crave and,
Of course your owner is a brilliant person who,
I quite like that's why I see you,
So I can be with her and be about her I tried to push,
Her from my mind but still she stays in,
My mind someone who I will never forget like custard,
On my shirt.

Could this be love?

I see you standing there looking at me and smiling at me your face so pearly and shiny with glee.

Then I see your eyes so wide and so bright they are truly a beautiful sight,
I get lost in them; they remind me of a flight to the moon amongst the starry night.
I see you standing there looking at me a radiant glow around your body a angel in disguise,
Something I do not despise.

Then I get your fragrance, soft and sweet like the smell of a thousand rose petals in a gentle beam of sunlight which then seems to dance and beat around my nostrils.

I see you standing there looking at me, staring directly into my eyes,
We don't blink for minutes despite the passing creatures, clouds and flies.

Finally I hear your voice a calm whisper,
Without a quiver or jitter,
A sound which will never die will never tire,
And will never disappear,
Every sentence is like a song from the most exotic of songbird from the heavens,
As you touch me with the lightest of strokes with the softest hands I feel the deepest of tickles,
And the most intense warm feeling a man could have,
And I wonder could this be love?

James Michael Davies

Dear grandad

There was a time you were full of life,
But then an illness made you bad,
You didn't give up and did fight,
Then an operation came along which made everyone glad,
Now you are once more the grandad I remember extremely
active and does never surrender,
The love and respect I have for you I have always had and will
last forever,
And I know you will get better.

Donnie

When you are near me I feel you deep,
Early on a morning before the birds sing I watch you sleep,
Every time we kiss and snuggle my heart does and will always leap.

I love the way you wear your hair,
I love the way you lovingly stare,
I love how we are so alike,
I love our time on a night.

You make me smile everyday,
The way you rarely get angry,
The way your papers are always tidy,
I love everything about you even when you alphabeticalise everything.

Your eyes bright as stars,
You are truly gorgeous.

James Michael Davies

Gone bad

The relationship changes from skies of blue bunnies of fluff and grass of green,
Now none can be compared as these have all gone and been.

The only thing that is now present is black clouds in a violent tornado of misery and pain,
The rabbits are bare and scared amongst the brown grass which was once green and it's unclear on who is to blame.

As they stare into each others hollow eyes words fly from her mouth as daggers would,
"Your love is niggardly and your feelings are scanty"
Which leads to him censure their whole aggregate since their first date.

Suddenly it becomes obvious that he was a tyrant and used to be very physical she stands there bruised and empty.

Until she finally, slowly turns away and walks cautiously and gently,
He drives away in his Bentley,
Love at first is summer but can end up like winter often reflecting those involved and their background as nothing but dark, cold and riddled with lies.

Heart

My happy blood red, beating heart,
Is now a depressed black throbbing,
Once my warm heart made sounds of joy and kept me going,
Now it's cold and simply creaks with a desperate effort which
keeps me back like I'm tied down with a rope of misery.

They say it will change in time,
Things will seem better,
Things will become easier,
My hearts says you lie,
My head says your right.

James Michael Davies

It all started with . . .

It all started with your glasses the way you wear them, they
way you look at me with your beautiful eyes.

I was instantly taken in we went on a date and I got hooked
on you,
Your personality is the most effective addictive drug in the
world and I can't get enough of you.

We got back to your place,
It was very modern and ace,
You slipped away for a bit what will happen next,
You came back even sexier we had the best sex!

It wasn't long before we went to church,
In order to make our lives merge,
Our marriage is still going strong,
We have even got our own song,
A shell is placed on our bedside,
To remind us of our honeymoon.

Morning beauty

The morning light breaks through my curtains,
As the beam of sun cuts into the atmosphere,
I am glad that we are both here.

I lay gazing at the ceiling,
I listen to the peace it's a unique feeling,
I rub out the sleep from my eyes,
And turn to my side.

You lay there,
The sunlight playing amongst your hair,
The radiant glow caressing your cheek,
Lying there totally still, quiet, asleep.

Your skin as soft,
As the breast of a finch.

James Michael Davies

Summer nights

We lay side by side beneath the beating sun,
As we relax together we are too content to run,
Instead we walk hand in hand to the tree-house to absorb the shade,
This is our special place because it is something we made.

We reach the top observe the scene and kiss,
Something extremely bliss,
This is where I give you a ring,
It makes you smile it makes me happy it makes the bluebirds sing.

Still we sit your head on my chest my hand on your breast,
From here we watch horse eat grass and the swallows nest,
On the horizon we see smoke,
Its people feasting from a BBQ and drinking coke.

As the sky turns to the colour mango,
We try to ignore it but know we must go,
As it is the end of today but we will meet tomorrow.

When hearts collide

I have an item as many can see it means a lot too me I exchanged it for my own as a promise that our love will grow, a heart.

It keeps me company when we are apart as it contains all the love, joy and happiness a man can hold.

The heart is not mine it belongs to another,
My lover,
As she has mine and I have hers our beating hearts is all I hear,
I have this feeling without the aid of beer,
The feeling of love.

Every time I see you my heart begins to skip, jump and dance be still my beating heart as stars may die,
Rivers may dry,
But the love between us will never exile.

The one i refer to as my love came down to me with wings of a dove with eyes so bright and skin so soft her name is . . . .

James Michael Davies

You and me

This is amazing you and me happy together always forever,
The feeling we get there is nothing better they may say,
"You've never met her"
"Just walk out the door" I say I will meet her there is nothing I
want more and there is no door.

I have a plan it will work but I need time something we have
lots of so never mind,
You are down there I'm up here I cant concentrate I keep
thinking of meeting her.

Then one day I do it I go there and see her, the experience
overwhelms me so radiant, so glorious, so beautiful we spend
days together,
Moments that last forever this is the day from here the real
beginning.

A empty success

They seem to have it all,
But they want more,
The money they withhold means they have it all?

Their house, open plan, white, isolated,
Outside, an edging of pure, fresh, lush green quaking grass
surrounds their living space,
Each blade plays amongst the steady summer breeze,
Calm,
But they want more.

Inside, modern, sterile, quiet,
A table of translucent alabaster stands next to open French
sliding doors,
The sweet aroma of juniper and rose Otto drifts in from the
clean, empty night,
But they want more.

Sapphire tiles lay on the floor of the stainless steel kitchen in
the company of a rare, precious oil painting,
Their garden contains hornbeam and ginkgo trees with patches
of spearmint plants carpeting their base,
But they want more.

James Michael Davies

They more as the albatross fly overhead,
Where no rodents run underfoot,
But,
While they get deliveries of fresh Brazil nut,

Friends are replaced with greed and ignorance as their drive
for money has left them alone,
They have everything but nothing.

A great pretender

He strides into view wearing cashmere,
He struts about in shoes of leather,
That's what he says, that's what we hear,
But we know that's not what we see,
Even though he does buzz like a bee.

He drives about in a jaguar,
He pays for petrol with cards of plastic,
That's what he shows, that's what we see,
But that's not what we know,
Children of four even know more.

He dines in only the best,
With a good looking lady on his arm,
They both ignore the rest,
Acting like this will only bring harm.

The cashmere and leather he wears is fake,
The jaguar he drives is stolen from his father,
The cards he is using are not his, fraud,
The dinner is a sham,
The lady is his sister not very glam.

James Michael Davies

Nezza

Their once was a fella called Nezza,
He thought their was nobody better,
Until dog matter filled his umbrella.

He was always clean after a was,
It made him feel rather posh.

Suddenly it started raining,
He had no idea his umbrella would fail him,
In his usual shower their was water and a chair where he would sit,
Then outside he was exposed to not a shower of water but a shower of . . . .

Nezza—bully?

This is another story about Nezza,
He has been making fun of a girl; he's never met her,
"You stink and never think" Is one of the things he says,
Much to the onlookers amaze!

He would thin of ways to make her cry,
But he only ever made her sigh,
Out of pity,
She thinks he is quite annoying and rather silly.

She decides to make a stand so that he will fall,
He explains that she can't and he will bounce back like a ball,
Nezza is a average white fella and not very loud,
So making fun of people helps him feel proud,
She starts to hunt him down to make him frown,
She is a massive lass and also brown.

She found Nezza,
The consequences were explosive she nearly changed him from a fella,
She picked him up and bounced him off the wall, floor and door,
Now Nezza is nice to big girls and eats hospital food a lot more!

The doctor: on a call

One lonely doctor carries hope on his shoulders,
The early morning sun glares off the windows,
His long heavy bag sits within his grip,
An unhealthy patient calls him out for this trip.

He stands at her door and puts on his public face,
A relative opens and is relieved by his grace,
He walks slowly up each step,
To the patient lying in bed.

He then sees her lying so still and grey,
Her eyes seem to change from what they once were,
She has survived this long through pure will,
The doctor gives her hope and comfort,
To her carer a discreet unhopeful view.

Before he leaves he fills the house with glorious hope,
confidence and dignity,
As the door closes he takes his first steps,
Back to the quiet he likes best,
And his broad sinking shoulders take weight once more.

The Taxman

Dawn breaks,
As the sun creeps,
From behind the house roofs, light streaks,
Across the streets.

A lone figure walks,
Eyes like a hawk`s,
And a face of no remorse,
As his chilling shadow stalks.

As the sun gets higher,
The sky lights up red and orange as if on fire,
The glow so intense his polished shoes gleam,
His leather shoes ring, along his path the gleam seems to light up his laces and seam.

Nobody wants to see this figure,
As he always sends you a quiver.

James Michael Davies

The return of the Taxman

A confident lone detached house,
Stands tall and proud wit smoke drifting from its spout,
Surrounded by fields and trees,
To the eye it does please.

Until the overlooking sky turns from blue to black,
A single figure walks with a long coat and a dark trilby hat,
As the house realizes the taxman is back.

As he goes closer to the large oak door,
The paint appears to peel and fall to the floor,
His leather gloves squeak beneath his tightened fist,
He banged three times against the wood,
Behind the door a shaking shadow is stood.

The Taxman: in the flesh

A typical street house stood,
Frames and doors made of wood,
Outside a glistening car with a canvas roof.

Inside Jack walked across his new flooring,
Feeling confident of the morning,
As he walked past his doorway,
There were three bangs close, a calling?

He opened the door carelessly,
To his horror there stood he,
His trilby hat casting a shadow,
Only revealing a grin from a mouth so narrow.

All dressed in black grasping his briefcase,
Jack looked back straight and changed his face,
Both men looked confident,
These two foes always did.

From his briefcase the Taxman produced paperwork,
Jack grasped the papers from his tight cold grip,
Took one look and begun to rip.

The chilling figures grin begun to fade,
As he realised the mistake he made,
Jack felt superior and full of glee,
Because the savings in his ISA are tax free.

James Michael Davies

The taxman: taxable surprise

There is a family that never worked,
Never moved,
Never cared,
There is a house that's grungy, grubby and dripping with gruel.

A dark figure enters the large garden,
Past the broken wall and between the stone griffins,
As he swiftly walks down the crumbled pathway,
The long thistles catch and attach to his long woven coat.

The ground crunches beneath each tailored shoe,
As he continues the sturdy trees, weeds and grass seem to move.

He knocks three times as the door gave way,
It slammed to the floor as the dust revealed,
A spotless interior with lavish luxuries,
(And a swimming pool so the kids can play)
The figure smiled with grim surprise issued a noticed and signed goodbye.

The Taxman: Alone

Within a country, within a street, within a house,
There is a large room with dark oak flooring,
And an open fire roaring,
And one alone Taxman ignoring.

Slumped in his armchair single malt in hand,
A stack of paperwork at his side,
He picks up one and a smile he can not hide,

A struggling family with five kids,
He decides they must pay more taxes,
His staring eyes gaze back to the flames,
And he decides to visit them in a few days.

James Michael Davies

A salmons struggle

Once their was a salmon who worked all day and night,
The thought of not working gave him a fright,
He battled and battled all his life,
Despite the warnings from the trouble and strife.

He would fight the water constantly all his days,
In many different ways,
And so he reaches the top of the waterfall,
After all these years of battling,
The trouble and strife thought it was very flattering,
And he was absolutely won out and died.

A win for the underdog

A dusty squirrel runs fast from a pile of logs,
Followed closely by a pack of dogs,
Running swiftly from tree to tree,
A bright red flash is all we see.

Over some nettles and past a stump a pack of three loses one,
They stop at a sudden and the stealthy squirrel seemed to be gone.

From the safety of a branch he sees two dogs turn into one,
As the owner whistles to come along,
Finally one canine sees his prey,
Eye to eye they both glare.

But the critter,
Proved to be wittier,
And left the gormless greyhound,
Simply hanging around,
From a hidden hunter's net disguised in the ground.

Ancient animals in the garden

Think all the dinosaurs are dead,
Think again,
One of their closest relatives is always in front of you,
Doing the simplest things.

Sifting and gliding as if in water,
Sitting proud as if they own,
Talking loud as if in a match,
Sitting on houses in groups of hundred.

Suddenly fleeing from the seagull, crow or starling,
Into my garden where there is water for them,
All over the lawn when the bath is full,

Someone makes a sound by dropping a cup.
They think they are being watched,
Gone in a flash not one left,
And another cup down,
They won't gather like that again till this time tomorrow.

That's when ill next see a dinosaur in my garden.

Beach life

Still, quiet, sandy lays the beach,
Empty cans and fag ends litter, what a cheek,
A great tit flutters down, the fag end rolls into his beak.

Outstanding!

The carelessness of man forms the security of nests so neat,
This bird has fags all day within his beak,
But can still sing a call so sweet.

One day he thinks enough!
He finishes the nest with twigs so rough,
And things as soft as fluff.

Still quiet lays the beach,
In the background the sky and sea meet,
The sun plays amongst the sand as it comes through blue
skies,
Encouraging more tits to venture and eat the flies.

James Michael Davies

Black red finned shark

Lurking under a rock,
His piercing stare looking at every fish,
His slow cold movement sloshing through the bubbled water,
He attacks any dying fish,
Truly the tough guy of the tank.

Discus (king of the aquarium fishes)

King of the fishes,
King of the colours,
King of the tank,
But not king of the community,
He stays by himself refusing to blend in,
His friends are the same species brown, blue, turquoise are the colours,
But no crushes.

James Michael Davies

Guppy

The guppy is the yuppie of the tank,
Likes the water to be clean and not rank,
Any quick changes and he gets upset and start nipping,
And his posh front starts slipping.

Bright red, yellow, brown are some of his colours,
Softly slipping through the water,
Showing off his beautiful colours,
Regular breeding is his way of living.

Khuli loach

The khuli loach is a strange sort of fellow,
Likes to be with mates at night,
But during the day his long snake like body likes to chill and
relax,
In the comfort of the shade and warmth,
Other fishes struggle to keep up,
And don't really know whether he is coming or going,
He is a happy speedy fish who tackles the game called life.

James Michael Davies

My fish

I love fish,
Tropical fish,
I keep them in a tank its relaxing to watch them at night,
Better than T.V.

Guppies, mollies, Platy, swordtails,
Happily swimming around safely,
Better than IPOD.

I am keeping them safe from dangerous weather,
And hunters and bigger fish,
Better than computers.

My pet

You're there when I'm happy,
You're there when I'm sad,
You chew on my slipper which makes me mad,
But when you bring me a paper I give you a pat.

Your golden brown hair glows in the sun,
And billows in the wind as a caramel river would.

You drink from a bowl,
And chase your ball,
I treat you like a god,
Because you are my spoilt dog.

James Michael Davies

Neon tetra

Fancy fins little size hard and picky at breeding,
Likes being in groups,
Can be like troops,
But can get bullied by sharks,
But can loose them by lark,
And sharp movements allow them to enjoy life.

When in groups there colours light up the tank,
And they become a real asset to its environment,
Because it makes the tank look like a underwater disco,
And anyone can go as long as hey glow.

Our pets

Pets, pets, pets
Should we keep them?
Should we not,
Should we release them?
Should we not.

Furry, hairy, fluffy,
Is it kind?
Is it not,
Is it evil?
Is it not.

James Michael Davies

Platy

Sunburst, sunset slowly stroll,
Mickey Mouse, marigold look for gold,
Small and colourful can breed at a flutter.

But subtle little and light,
For an amateur is just right,
Shy but just slight swims through water like its flying,
An honest fish it knows no lying.

Socially happy and always on the go,
If I were to ask him to slow he would say no,
And as he lives and has a good feed,
He realises he must breed.

Scrounging pigeons

First there is nothing totally still as the sea on a warm summers day,
Until,
Somebody carelessly throws a half eaten pasty on the floor,
Suddenly a flying troop swooshes down from the heavens and squabble and fight over this nourish treat and its every bird for themselves.

Feathers and noise increase as the group grows and grows the ones closest to the edge become more and more desperate for something to eat so these become the most vicious the pasty spreads along the floor as the group disperses.

Each individual wrestles another beak to beak the hard hook shaped beaks furiously attack the food, eventually the food dwindles and dwindles until there is a instant lack of hurrying pink coral claws then the food is gone.

The objective has been completed by the troops the target has been exterminated as they return to their posts along rooftops and bus shelters unsatisfied with there meal, they await for another but for now the high street is as still as a frozen lake but for how long will these feathered assassins wait before they decide to scrounge again.

James Michael Davies

Swordtail

Long sharp black and white tail,
Pointing behind as if it's a trail,
Which the females pick up on and follow,
As he cuts through the warm waters,
Looking for them until realising he has a trail of them behind
him.

And like a shooting star with speed and colour,
He picks one it doesn't take him long,
He then has all the components to show himself off.

The crow

Hanging around picking at carcass,
Hovering staring stalking marks the prey.

Swooping diving meal of the day,
Whatever the weather come what may,
Spooky dark but collected.

Feathers like leathers,
Wings like wheels,
In groups of attitude,
They know no rules.

The crow is a character of his own,
The biker is a character of his own,
Bikes and prey go along,
They are masters and sing no song.

James Michael Davies